Vocabulary

Introductory Pupil Book

Louis Fidge and Sarah Lindsay

William Collins' dream of knowledge for all began with the publication of his first book in 1819. A self-educated mill worker, he not only enriched millions of lives, but also founded a flourishing publishing house. Today, staying true to this spirit, Collins books are packed with inspiration, innovation and practical expertise. They place you at the centre of a world of possibility and give you exactly what you need to explore it.

Collins. Freedom to teach.

Acknowledgements
p9, top left: Knaupe/iStockphoto; p9, bottom left: Knaupe/iStockphoto; p9, top right: Konstantin Petkov; p9, bottom right: Knaupe/iStockphoto.

Published by Collins
An imprint of HarperCollins*Publishers* Ltd.
77–85 Fulham Palace Road
Hammersmith
London
W6 8JB

**Browse the complete Collins catalogue at
www.collinseducation.com**

Text © Louis Fidge and Sarah Lindsay 2013
Design and illustrations © HarperCollins*Publishers* Limited 2013

Previously published as *Collins Primary Writing*, first published 1998; and *Collins Focus on Writing*, first published 2002.

10 9 8 7 6 5 4 3 2 1

ISBN: 978-0-00-750099-4

Louis Fidge and Sarah Lindsay assert their moral right to be identified as the authors of this work.

British Library Cataloguing in Publication Data
A Catalogue record for this publication is available from the British Library.

Cover template: Laing & Carroll
Cover illustration: Paul McCaffrey
Series design: Neil Adams
Picture research: Gill Metcalfe
Illustrations: James Walmesley and Sue Woollatt
Some illustrations have been reused from the previous edition (978-0-00-713206-5).

Printed and bound by Printing Express Limited, Hong Kong.

Contents

Abdullah

Numbers and colours

Number words

1	**2**	**3**	**4**	**5**
one	two	three	four	five
6	**7**	**8**	**9**	**10**
six	seven	eight	nine	ten

Colour words

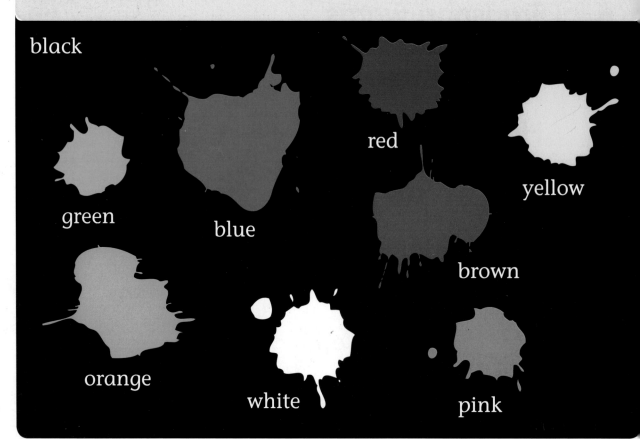

black

red

yellow

green

blue

brown

orange

white

pink

Practice

1. Copy the sentences. Choose a number word to fill the gap.

   ✓ a) A dog has ___four___ legs.

   b) There are ___seven___ days in a week.

   c) Five plus four is ___nine___.

2. Copy the sentences. Choose a colour word to fill the gap.

   ✓ a) A lemon is ___yellow___.

   b) The mud we played in made us ___brown___.

   c) The ___red___ blood dripped down my knee.

More to think about

Look at each picture. Write a sentence about each one. Each sentence must use a colour word and a number word.

1.

2.

3.

4.

Use the words in the box to match with the correct numbers.

| eleven | twelve | thirteen | fourteen | fifteen |
| sixteen | seventeen | eighteen | nineteen | twenty |

1. 15 _fifteen_
2. 19 _nineteen_
3. 12 _twelve_
4. 20 _twenty_
5. 13 _thirteen_
6. 16 _sixteen_

Look at the picture. Write down in words how many kilometres it is to the pool. 6km _SIX Km_

These are the **days of the week**.

Monday
Tuesday
Wednesday
Thursday
Friday
Saturday
Sunday

These are the **months of the year**.

January
February
March
April
May
June
July
August
September
October
November
December

Practice

Copy the words. Write the next month or day next to each one.

1. Wednesday _Thursday_
2. Monday _tuesday_
3. March _April_
4. September _october_
5. Friday _saturday_
6. Sunday _Monday_
7. July _agust_
8. December _January_

Friday

Saturday

Sunday

More to think about

Write down the answers to these questions.

1. Which day comes before Tuesday?
2. Which month comes after November?
3. Which two days make the weekend?
4. Which is your favourite month? Why?
5. Which is your favourite day? Why?
6. In which month is your birthday?

Look at the pictures of these trees.
They show different seasons.
Write the months in which you'd find each tree.

1.

2.

3.

4.

Body words

All these words are **parts of the head**.

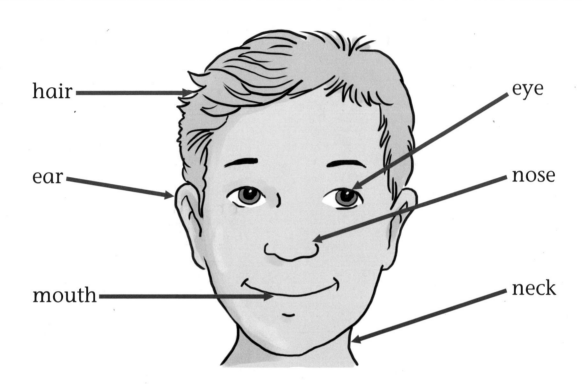

hair

eye

ear

nose

mouth

neck

Practice

Copy the sentences.
Choose the correct word to fill the gap.

1. I smell with my <u>nose</u>.
2. I hear with my <u>ear</u>.
3. I see with my <u>eye</u>.
4. I eat with my <u>hana</u>.
5. On top of my head I have <u>hair</u>.
6. My head is joined to my body by my <u>heck</u>.

More to think about

Find the hidden words. They all name parts
of the body. Make a list.

1. acb**arm**degh
2. lkjhandipkm
3. zchestvdqwk
4. vcxzakneeo
5. footdsawyug
6. hjfanklewer
7. zshoulderxh
8. jklelbowmb
9. qwertylegac
10. wristyuoph

Now try these

Look at the picture. Copy out the numbers in the picture.
Write down the names of parts of the body next to each
number. Name the part of the body.

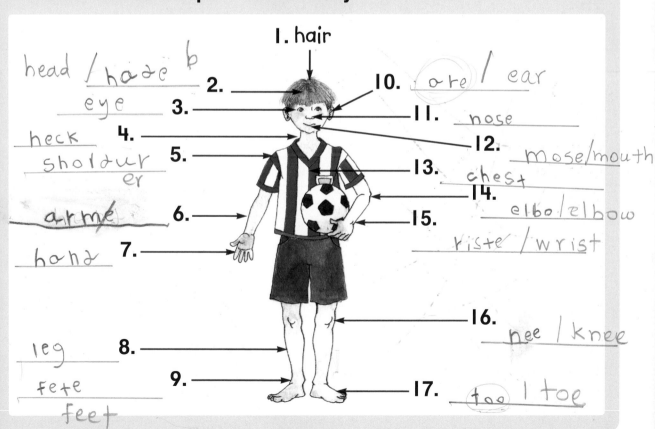

1. hair

head / haee b
2.
eye 3.
heck 4.
sholdur 5.
er
arme 6.
hand 7.
leg 8.
fete 9.
feet

10. ore / ear
11. nose
12.
mose/mouth
13. chest
14.
elbo/elbow
15.
riste / wrist

16.
nee / knee
17. too / toe

Antonyms

Antonyms are words with **opposite meanings**.
These words are **antonyms**.

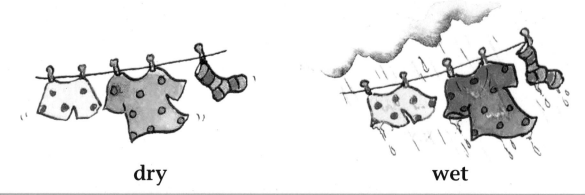

dry   wet

Practice

Copy these word lists. Match each word with its antonym by joining them with a line.

old   long

clean   poor

short   young

fat   shut

rich   dull

shiny   thin

open   dark

light   dirty

More to think about

Find the hidden antonyms. Make a list.

1. dry ⟶ ab**wet**cde
2. quick ⟶ f**slow**ghij
3. small ⟶ **big**klmnop
4. cold ⟶ qrstu**hot**v
5. happy ⟶ wxs**ad**yzab
6. soft ⟶ gk**hard**mn

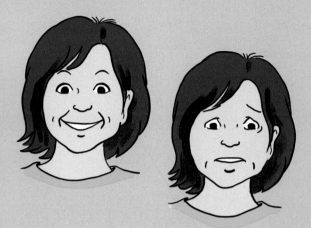

Now try these

Copy the sentences. Write an antonym for the underlined word.

1. Tara is not <u>weak</u>.
   She is <u>strong</u>____.

2. Ben is not <u>awake</u>.
   He is _____.

3. I <u>love</u> ice cream but
   I _____ cabbage.

4. The scissors are <u>blunt</u>
   so we need _____ ones.

5. My glass is <u>empty</u> but
   your glass is _____.

6. Grandma is an <u>old</u> lady.
   Sue is a _____ girl.

Unit 5 — Compound words

A **compound word** is two small words joined together.

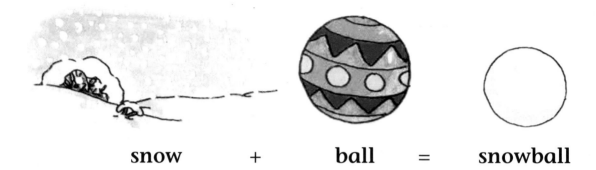

snow   +   ball   =   snowball

Practice

Join the small words together.
Write the compound word.

1. snow + man = *snowman*

2. hand + bag = *handbag*

3. tea + spoon = *teaspoon*

4. sun + light = *sunlight*

5. foot + ball = *football*

6. air + port = *airport*

More to think about

Copy the compound word.
Then write its two short words.

1. rainbow   = __rain__ + __bow__
2. eyelid   = __eye__ + __lid__
3. afternoon   = __after__ + __noon__
4. everything   = __every__ + __thing__
5. lunchtime   = __lunch__ + __time__
6. someone   = __some__ + __one__

Now try these

1. Write the compound word.

a) [image] + [image]   = __raindrop__

b) [image] + [image]   = __toothbrush__

c) [image] + [image]   = __earing__

d) [image] + [image]   = __sandcastle__

2. Write a sentence for each compound word.

15

These words are **connected**. They are all **means of transport**.

bus	bicycle	car
train	aeroplane	boat

Practice

Copy the sentences. Choose the correct word from above to complete each sentence.

1. A (car/boat) has four wheels.

2. An (ship/aeroplane) flies in the sky.

3. A (boat/bike) floats on water.

4. A (tractor/bus) carries a lot of people.

5. A (rocket/coach) zooms into space.

6. A farmer rides a (rocket/tractor).

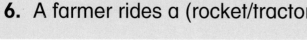

More to think about

Copy the table.
Write the words from the box in the correct columns.

land transport	sea transport	air transport

bus   aeroplane   boat   train   helicopter   bicycle
lorry   glider   rocket   raft   yacht   submarine

Now try these

1. Copy the words. Circle the first letter of each word.
   Write the words in alphabetical order.

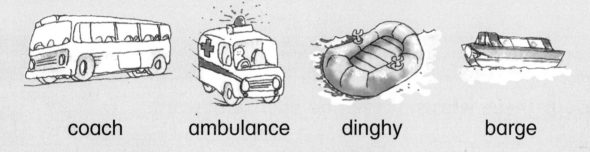

coach   ambulance   dinghy   barge

2. Write these words in alphabetical order.

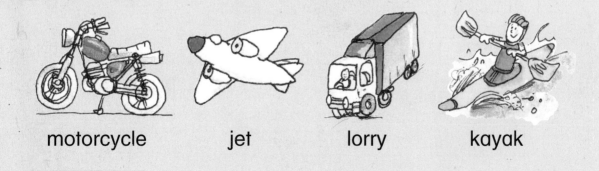

motorcycle   jet   lorry   kayak

A **root word** is a word that a prefix or suffix is added to.

The meaning of a root word changes when a prefix or suffix is added.

A **prefix** is a group of letters added to the **beginning** of a root word.

untie =   un   +   tie

        ↑   ↑
    (prefix)   (root word)

A **suffix** is a group of letters added to the **end** of a root word.

helpful =   help   +   ful

            ↑   ↑
        (root word)   (suffix)

Practice

Copy these words. Underline each root word.

1.
unlock

2.
unhappy

3.
careful

4.
unzip

5.
painful

6.
lovely

More to think about

Add the prefix to the root word.

1. un + kind = _unkind_

2. un + tidy = _untidy_

3. un + fair = _unfair_

Add the suffix to the root word.

1. aim + less = _aimless_

2. care + less = _careless_

3. end + less = _endless_

Now try these

1. Choose a suffix from the box to make a new word using the root word. Write out the new words you make.

ment	ness	ful

a) enjoy_ment_   b) help_ful_   c) sad_ness_

d) excite_ness_   e) mean_ful_   f) mouth_ful_

2. Write four more words with the prefix **un**.

Homophones

Some words **sound the same** but have **different spellings and meanings**.

They are called **homophones**.

Say the words **blue** and **blew** aloud.

Practice

Write the correct homophones to match the pictures.
The words in the box will help.

rose   pear   son   meet   rows   pair   meat   sun

1.

2.

3.

4.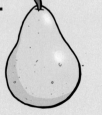

More to think about

Write the two homophones found in each list.

1. but   be   bite   bee   black   bad

2. hat   hair   house   hare   hello   hand

3. fish   frog   fur   feet   fist   fir

4. sun   see   sock   sea   sit   sand

5. ride   write   wren   right   river   wet

6. nose   knight   kick   night   knot   never

Now try these

1. Copy and finish the sentences.

   a) I ___rode___ down the ___road___ .
   (road/rode)

   b) We _____ _____ cakes!
   (eight/ate)

   c) She could _____ the _____
   from her house.
   (see/sea)

   d) The _____ balloon _____ in the wind.
   (blue/blew)

   e) Dan looked _____ his _____ mice.
   (for/four)

2. Write your own sentences using the homophones **buy**
   and **bye**.

21

Story words

All these **words** can be used to write a **story**.

woods

castle

princess

prince

horse

Practice

Match the beginning of each sentence to its ending.
Copy the sentences.

1. The giant was   magic spells.

2. A princess lived   in the woods.

3. The prince rode   her wand.

4. The magician made   very big.

5. The little fairy waved   a white horse.

6. The dragon played   in the castle.

More to think about

Write the words from the box that match each picture.

> a beautiful princess   a dark cave   a cunning fox
> an ugly troll   a tall tower   a thatched cottage
> a fat frog   a good fairy   a black cat

1.

2.

3.

4.

5.

6.

7.

8.

9.

Now try these

Copy the table. Write the words from the box
in the correct columns.

people	animals	places

> pirate   castle   fox   woodcutter   giant   lion
> forest   lake   queen   wolf   unicorn   mountain

Unit 10

Using interesting words

To make your writing better you can add **interesting words**.

The wind blew the hat.

The **strong** wind blew the **big** hat.

Which sentence is more interesting?

Practice

Use a word from the box to make each noun sound more interesting.

sunny	black	smelly	sweet

1.

The _____ dog

2.

A _____ day

3.

Some _____ apples

4.

A _____ sock

More to think about

Write your own interesting words to describe these nouns.

1. the _beautiful_ dress

2. the _____ boy

3. a _____ bird

4. some _____ chips

5. a _____ flower

6. the _____ book

Now try these

Copy these sentences and add interesting words.

1. I ran up the ___steep___ road to school.

2. Tim stroked the _____ cat.

3. We watched the _____ film.

4. The _____ drink was tasty.

5. The _____ stream was fun to play in.

6. Jess loved to play with the _____ ball.

Synonyms are words with **similar** meanings.

The words **happy** and **cheerful** are synonyms.

Tom was **happy** on his birthday. He felt **cheerful**.

Practice

Write a synonym from the box for each word.

| big | small | start | wet | quick | difficult |

1. tiny   _small_

2. fast   _____

3. begin   _____

4. huge   _____

5. hard   _____

6. damp   _____

More to think about

Copy the lists.
Underline the synonym for the first word in each list.

1. scared   hot   <u>frightened</u>   trees
2. finish   cat   book   end
3. sick   ill   grass   wet
4. happy   clever   low   joyful
5. foolish   day   silly   empty
6. sad   went   mop   unhappy

Now try these

Copy the pairs of sentences.
Choose a synonym from the box to complete
the second sentence in each pair.

dropped	thirsty	soon	cold	deaf

1. We'll go out to play in a short while.
   We'll go out to play ___*soon*___.

2. Shireen let the cup fall on the floor.
   Shireen _____ the cup on the floor.

3. The old lady cannot hear.
   The old lady is _____.

4. The dog needed a drink.
   The dog was _____.

5. The water was very chilly.
   The water was very _____.

Using clues

Pictures can sometimes give us **clues** to the **meaning of words**.

a queue

Practice

Match each picture with the correct word from the box.
Write out your answers.

| shark | tree | purse | gift | fence | skirt |

1.

2.

3.

4.

5.

6.

More to think about

Answer the questions in sentences.
The pictures will help you!

1. Is lunch ready?

2. Are the children sad?

3. Is he late for school?

4. Can she ride a bike?

Now try these

Write a sentence about each of these pictures.
Use interesting words.

1.

2.

3.

4.

Progress Unit

1. Copy the sentences.
   Use a colour or number word in each gap.

   a) A duck has _____ wings.

   b) You can eat a tomato when it is _____.

   c) Clouds can be _____ or _____.

   d) Seven add seven is _____.

2. Write the day or month to answer the questions below.

   a) Which day comes before Friday?

   b) Which month comes before May?

   c) Which day comes after Tuesday?

   d) Which month comes after August?

3. Write a part of the body that begins with the letter:

   a) a_____   b) e_____

   c) f_____   d) h_____

4. Match each word in Set A with its antonym in Set B.
   (opposite)

Set A	Set B
hot	short
fast	big
small	good
bad	cold
long	slow
sad	soft
hard	happy

5. Choose a word from the box to complete each compound word. Write out the compound words.

> **castle   spoon   ache   house   ball   drop**

a) tea   b) snow

c) tooth   d) green

e) rain   f) sand

6. Write two types of transport for each group.

a) Transport by **land**

b) Transport by **sea**

c) Transport by **air**

7. Copy the words. Underline the root words.

a) disobey   b) unwell

c) cupful   d) endless

8. Match each homophone with a word from the box.

> **tail   stare   hey   our**

a) hay   b) tale

c) hour   d) stair

9. Write and match the beginning of each
sentence with its correct ending.

a) A brown bear   chased a mouse.

b) The black cat   jumped in to the pond.

c) The beautiful princess   makes wishes come true.

d) Two fat frogs   lived in the big cave.

e) A good fairy   slept in the castle.

10. Write an interesting word to describe these nouns.

a) a _____ car   b) a _____ forest

c) a _____ rat   d) a _____ coat

11. Write a synonym for each word.

a) big   b) sad

c) cry   d) shout

e) fall   f) start

g) fast   h) tiny

i) lumpy   j) wet

12. Write a question you can ask about each picture.

 a)    b)    c)